ISTJ: 33 Secrets From The Life of an ISTJ

By Diana Jackson

Contents

ISTJ: Introverted, Sensing, Thinking, Judging

1. Tendency to be reserved

Positive: Reserve is a trait that stems from the introverted aspect of the ISTJ's personality, and it's what prevents this stand-up member of society from taking any brash action in the public eye – action which could have a damaging effect on their all-important reputation. ISTJs also deploy restrained politeness as a way of keeping unsavory characters at arm's length.

Negative: Despite being one of the most common personality types out there, ISTJs can be difficult to get to know by virtue of their introversion and their preference for fully analyzing someone before letting them into the tight circle of friends and family that ISTJs keep. Their reserved natures can end up seeming aloof or even arrogant to people who don't know them well.

In Relationships: ISTJs might have a tough time dating, but not because they have little to offer partners (they have tons!) but because they keep close to themselves and have a difficult time letting people enter their world in an intimate way. In order for ISTJs to make a love connection, they have to make the effort to be more outspoken when they have feelings for someone.

At Work: ISTJs are incredibly devoted employees who are the hardest-working people on staff, but they might miss out on employee group-lunches or not get the invite to hang out at the bar for happy hour, simply because they tend to shy away from mixing with the other people at work. It could take quite a while before they come out of their shell and behave more sociably on the job.

2. Completely reliable

Positive: If you ask your ISTJ friend for a lift home from the airport, not even an atomic bomb could keep them from fulfilling their promise. This personality type is so incredibly special because they are the people who never renege on their word, no matter what outside forces might try to complicate their honor. Without ISTJs, the world would be a much less dependable place.

Negative: The downside to this kind of reliability is that it's incredibly objective – ISTJs see things in black and white. They're the friend who witnessed you breaking the neighbor's window with a fly ball when you were kids, and they marched right up to the front door to inform the owners of what you did. They are just *so* straight-laced.

In Relationships: The easiest way to make a good impression on a first date? Not be late. And ISTJs have that on lock. Whatever stage the relationship is in, whether it's courtship or a marriage of 40-plus years, ISTJs are unwavering in their devotion and their willingness to do anything for the people they love (including dressing up in a ridiculous costume for the kids!).

At Work: Employers will come to absolutely love and depend upon their ISTJ employees, and ISTJs can expect to find that the combination of their hard work with their dependability is a powerful mixture that spells success. Bosses remember the guy or gal who is never late, who always gets the work in on time and who saves other people's butts in a pinch. Those people get raises and promotions.

3. Practical and realistic

Positive: If a job needs to be done, and it needs to be done efficiently, the sensing ISTJ has a definite edge over their INTJ counterpart. The shortest distance between two locations is a straight line, and ISTJs are always searching for that linear answer, because it solves problems effectively with the quickest possible turnaround.

Negative: Picture an ISTJ sent in to tell his tone-deaf 10-year-old niece that her dreams of becoming a world-famous singer are far-fetched, at best. You could expect a lot of tears from the one and a great deal of "I'm doing you a favor" from the other. ISTJs have a difficult time discerning between situations where their practicality/realism is an advantage, and where a little human tact is more appropriate.

In Relationships: Love is essential to relationship, but practicality and good sense make a marriage last. Whether it's holding off on having children until the parents are financially stable or even being able to recognize when the relationship is no longer working as it should, ISTJs can make the tough decisions that others whither and dither over for months or sometimes even years.

At Work: These two traits usually inform the type of work that ISTJs get into, which often puts them in professional careers – like law or accounting – but can lead them into fields like military service and detective work. ISTJs try to see and live in the world as it really is, and they often serve others with this POV.

4. Trustworthy

Positive: If you have a secret and you need to tell someone, your ISTJ best friend is a good bet. Unlike so many other people out there, ISTJs take the secrets they are told to the grave – such is the level of their trustworthiness. They are the people that help you believe characteristics like integrity and loyalty are still alive and kicking.

Negative: The downside is if you are the person opposite the ISTJ, and you need to know what they know. It would physically pain them to betray anyone's trust, and – who knows – they themselves could get hurt in the process of extraction. ISTJs are protectors, but the secrets they protect could be dangerous.

In Relationships: If you're married to an ISTJ, you can at least count on the fact that they really are working late – not having an illicit affair at some motel. In fact, marriage ranks among the ISTJs most important and valued institutions, so if they were going to shock the world and cheat at something, it would be taxes before spouse.

At Work: Their reputation for discretion gives employers the confidence to trust ISTJs with sensitive information, so this personality type can find themselves rising through the ranks with relative ease. They aren't flashy people, by any means, but they stand out from among their peers by virtue of their strongly held virtues.

5. Prefers solitude

Positive: Like any true introvert, ISTJs would just rather be alone. Since this is how they "recharge their batteries," seeking solitude helps this personality type to re-enter the world refreshed and composed. ISTJs also value the many benefits of giving themselves time and space to think about the important decisions in their lives before taking action.

Negative: People who spend a lot of time on their own can end up incredibly isolated, and, in worst-case scenarios, they might develop depression. Humans are social and communal creatures who need interaction for overall good health, and ISTJs can set themselves up for mental health issues which can turn into physical ailments if left untreated.

In Relationships: ISTJ partners hopefully weren't expecting to spend every waking moment with their mate, because that would drive this personality type up a wall (to say nothing about killing the relationship entirely). If ISTJs are smart, they will find someone equally independent, who is happy to regularly pursue his/her own interests without clinginess or neediness.

At Work: ISTJs look for careers where they can be trusted to work with relative autonomy (and it would be shocking news that someone might *not* trust them). This personality type doesn't mind having coworkers, though, as long as the boundaries are clearly defined and there won't be anyone interfering or being meddlesome. The ISTJ preference for solitude also leads them toward freelance positions.

6. Completes tasks using logic and reason

Positive: Using logic and reason to complete a task – whether it's building a desk from Walmart or performing surgery – just makes sense, and the ISTJ values sense very highly. This enables them to do the work at hand with great efficiency and accuracy – no taking apart and re-assembling due to error is necessary if the ISTJ is leading the project, at home, at work or anywhere.

Negative: But if the task at hand requires consoling a grieving friend...what then? The ISTJ is at a bit of a loss, and their discomfort and awkwardness as they find themselves adrift in mysterious waters, can end up making matters worse. Logic and reason are well and good, but matters of the heart that need resolving call for a response that is empathic and caring.

In Relationships: As a spouse in a house, ISTJs are the best to have around. These keenly penetrating personality types can look at any issue – a leaky pipe, a cluttered junk room, that dangerously packed closet – and figure out the best way to fix it in the least amount of time. And ISTJs aren't procrastinators, either – they get stuff done ASAP, leaving more time later for fun couples' or family activities.

At Work: Because of their penchant for logic and reason, ISTJs excel in sciences and mathematics, but their cool, pragmatic demeanor is also effective in writing careers like journalism. And tasks doesn't just mean work projects – if their workspace starts to get messy, they'll have it neat as a pin in no time (so that they can get right back to work, of course).

7. Likes to make things orderly and organized

Positive: ISTJs don't just think about how life would be better if it were more organized – they do it. And no project is too big for their determination and enthusiasm – that is to say, ISTJs not only have the impulse to organize, they really love doing it. ISTJs can't control everything, but they do have autonomy over their immediate environment.

Negative: A little organization and orderliness is definitely a good thing, but ISTJs have the capacity to take it into obsessive-compulsive disorder territory. Not everything can be put into its proper place – take people, for example, who operate of their own free will and won't be told what to do all the time – and ISTJs' frustrations can bubble over, when they just need to relax.

In Relationships: From their weekend schedule to the sock drawers, ISTJs like having things planned out. If they try to date someone on the perceiving end of the spectrum, it could end very badly. However, another judging type would not only appreciate their ISTJ's wonderful organizational skills, they would complement it.

At Work: A place for everything at their desk, as well as an orderly procedure on the job – those are the hallmarks of the ISTJ employee, and it's what makes them such great, dependable professionals. Their talent for organization often puts ISTJs in the upper tiers of management, and though they don't relish bossing people around, seeing the work get done in an efficient manner is very satisfying for ISTJs.

8. Respects traditions and loyalty

Positive: Of all the personality types, the ISTJ is the one with the deepest and most abiding respect for tradition. This makes them pillars of the community and devoted family members, and it makes the world a more stable, secure place for everyone else to be. Thanks to ISTJs, chivalry, manners and integrity haven't fallen completely by the wayside.

Negative: The disadvantages of valuing tradition too strongly can be seen in the violent conflicts that arise between people of different cultures, races or religions. If taken to their limits, the ideas of tradition and loyalty can also be exclusionary and biased, leading to close-minded cultures that bully, ostracize and ignore. Because they have a hard time seeing gray area, ISTJs can inadvertently take part in prejudice or bigotry.

In Relationships: Though the ISTJ isn't much of a dreamer, this personality nonetheless has known all his or her life what kind of family they desired. It's the white-picket-fence-2.5-kids-and-a-dog kind of life that appeals to them, and you can bet that when they take their marriage vows they say "forever" and they mean it, 100 percent. It's a rare sentiment anymore, but it's an admirable one.

At Work: Pass a petition to the ISTJ coworker and expect to see him or her pass it right along without a second glance. ISTJs wouldn't have come to work for a company if they thought it needed to be changed. For them, the traditions of their workplace are likely part of what brought them there in the first place. So dissent all you like, but don't expect the ISTJ to take up signs and join the picket line.

9. Enjoys a quiet, peaceful environment

Positive: Serenity and calm – that's the kind of environment where people can think, muse or make important decisions, and it's the one that ISTJs prefer to find themselves in. Surprisingly, they are good in moment of crisis or panic, but if they had their choice, ISTJs would always inhabit quiet, peaceful locales that allow them to be the very best versions of themselves.

Negative: Would that we all could control our environments, but that is simply not the case. We have to handle what life throws at us, and if that happens to involve a crowded grocery store line with a bunch of screaming, crying babies, well, it's on us to keep our cool and not make snide comments under our breath. Can ISTJs hold it in? For the most part, but they might unfairly take out their annoyance on the store clerk.

In Relationships: If you met an ISTJ at a dance club, you might want to have them re-take the MBTI test. This personality type would rather spend a quiet evening in, making dinner with their sweetie before curling up on the couch for a movie. Club-hoppers need not apply – the ISTJ isn't going to budge on crowded venues with blasting music.

At Work: One of the reasons ISTJs are happy freelancing is because they work with total independence and they can do so from whatever location fits. Don't be surprised if the ISTJ freelancer has a home office with a door that shuts and locks, as well as a soothing mini-waterfall and aromatherapy candles to increase concentration.

10. Places high premium on security

Positive: Security comes in all forms – financial security, job security, relationship security – and the ISTJ seeks it all. In so doing they create a world around them that is more stable and secure for everyone else – a positive ripple effect from which everyone benefits, whether they realize it or not. ISTJs are the backbone of any functioning society, and we are lucky to have personality types like this quietly doing what needs to be done.

Negative: As important as security is, there are a lot of other factors which should be considered, and the ISTJ's limited perspective can often leave them emotion-blind. Further, people who become obsessed with security can also become paranoid, making it difficult for them to relate to anyone else and giving them an unpleasantness that will drive people away.

In Relationships: The ISTJ might not say the sweet, lovey-dovey words from a rom-com to his or her partner, but they show how much they care by providing for the ones they love – in full measure. Anyone with an ISTJ has got to understand that love is a show, not tell emotion, but mates paying attention to the ISTJ's actions will understand the depth of their feelings from the commitment displayed every day.

At Work: Even freelancing ISTJs are going to work as hard as possible to have a career that allows them to provide for themselves and their families. ISTJs certainly have professional passions, but a job will always be, at least partly, a means to an

end. This is why ISTJs are able to work jobs that they hate –
they remind themselves of why they're doing it: stability and
security in a world fraught with unknown quantities.

11. Has a strong sense of duty

Positive: When a friend says she will go to a boring event with you, which yourself are under obligation to attend, and then she backs out at the last minute, well – you know then and there she is not an ISTJ. Through situations both minor and dire, the ISTJ is imbued with the sense that doing the right thing is the only thing. No bailing, no questions.

Negative: But what about duty that crosses the line? What if the accountant ISTJ's unethical boss asks him/her to cook the books, just for a few months? (No one will notice.) What if the soldier ISTJ is asked to do something which goes against his or her moral beliefs? These types of situations don't happen often, but when/if they do, the ISTJ will be at an utter loss – perhaps for the first and only time.

In Relationships: Male ISTJs in particular will feel the weight of traditional values coming down heavily on their shoulders. This includes providing for their wife and family and heading up the household and making all the big decisions. It means that they will always put others ahead of themselves – again, as an expression of deep love and caring, where words don't come readily.

At Work: Staying later than everyone else to make sure the project is completed, helping others who are behind on their work or even cleaning out the break room fridge because something smells terrible...these are the types of things that the ISTJ employee is willing to do, because a company is only as good as the sum of its parts. If it's clearly defined as duty, the ISTJ is on it, without complaint.

12. Does not enjoy spontaneity

Positive: Spontaneity can be wasteful of both time and money, both of which, the ISTJ would reason, can be spent on worthier activities. It's true, though – the last time you did something spontaneous, it probably involved going out of your way for something and spending money you don't necessarily have. ISTJs practice a kind of self-control the rest of us can only dream about.

Negative: A little spontaneity can be good for the soul, though, especially if it's just dropping by a friend's house to chat while she recovers from surgery. But the ISTJ likes everything so orderly and planned out that it can be impossible to squeeze in anything fun. And a life without fun really isn't much of a life at all. It's all about balance, and the ISTJ has to actively try to achieve that balance.

In Relationships: ISTJs' mates better not expect surprise trips to the tropics or a gift on their pillow at night, because surprises are not going to be forthcoming from this most predictable of personality types. However, if ISTJ spouses want to make a date in advance, their partner will be there come hell or high-water.

At Work: Some judging types are actually quite mentally flexible, but the ISTJ resents spontaneity in the workplace in pretty much all of its forms. This includes having new projects sprung on them with short turnaround expectations or coming to work and finding that they have to train the new guy. ISTJs will do it – it's their duty – but you can expect some simmering resentment under the surface.

13. Follows things through to completion

Positive: A lot of people out there take up a project and then, for some reason, quit. Over and over again, we do this. But ISTJs finish what they start, and it's a good thing they're around to pick up the slack. How would it be if we had half-finished schools or restaurant food that came out half-frozen? ISTJs say, "Not good at all," and they put their heads down and do the job until it's done.

Negative: For a personality type that doesn't like to waste time, ISTJs' one weakness in that area is being unable to stop themselves from quitting something where it's pointless to go on. For them it's not pointless – but it's probably obvious to everyone else around them that they are beating against a current whose strength always overcomes.

In Relationships: One of the biggest complaints married couples have about each other is the "he started building our deck and then stopped" or "she began to paint the spare bedroom, but got distracted." The ISTJ home will always look its very best, because the ISTJ not only mentally organizes everything, he or she believes the job isn't done until the physical task has been completed: every room, every floor, even the closets.

At Work: Every boss's dream – the guy or gal who can take direction and then work incredibly hard until the project is complete. Not three-fourths of the way done, not "nearly there but not quite" – the ISTJ doesn't quit until the project is 100 percent finished, and even then it has to be finished to their exacting standards. This is often best accomplished when the ISTJ is working alone, not in groups.

14. Displays ready loyalty

Positive: If you have ever been in a situation where you should have spoken up on a friend's behalf but you didn't (for whatever reason), you can appreciate the ISTJ's willingness to display loyalty, even when it won't make them very popular. When it comes to traditions and values, ISTJs don't just talk the talk, they walk the walk. You could never accuse ISTJs of being hypocrites where their values are concerned.

Negative: Sometimes there are situations where the traditions or values to which the ISTJ can be loyal – this is usually quite a conservative bunch – are outdated or not in keeping with the changes that have swept through society. Regardless, the ISTJ will show their support, despite having friends or even family members who comprise the types of people who find themselves persecuted or excluded by the ISTJ's loyalty.

In Relationships: Taking a stand for their partner: that is the ISTJ way. Whether it's a rude waitress at a restaurant or a snotty colleague at a work function, if you step on the toes of the ISTJ's true love, you will feel their burn. As introverts, ISTJs usually slide away from conflict, but their protective alerts go off when it comes to their mates. Watch out – because the ISTJ can hit below the belt when they're angry.

At Work: The ISTJ wouldn't work for a specific company or business if they didn't feel that the mission of the enterprise didn't match their own (ISTJs do their research!). Those who have been with a company for a while will feel a particular loyalty to it, especially if they are on the receiving end of benefits and promotions. So anyone talking smack on their company in front of the ISTJ can expect to be "corrected" with a description of how wrong they are.

15. Values honesty and integrity

Positive: ISTJs are truly stand-up and stand-out citizens, the kinds of people who bring down crooks, liars and fakes. Because of their deeply-felt honesty and integrity, they always strive to do the right thing and to teach others to be the same. As introverted thinking types, ISTJs won't choose to work face-to-face with people; instead, they will simply lead by example.

Negative: For as hard-headed and seemingly hard-hearted as ISTJs can be, this is one naïve bunch when it comes to the motives of others. When faced with a dishonest boss or a cheating spouse, this personality type will be utterly railroaded by shock – it's so hard for them to imagine that the other people in the world don't share their same values. The disappointment they feel can really harden them emotionally.

In Relationships: ISTJ mates might feel as though they are dating some kind of saint. However, there must be some kind of matching personality traits in order for the ISTJ to give another person the time of day to begin with. And even when it comes to the hard topics, like "I don't think is working," the ISTJ would much rather hear the truth upfront, with respect and courtesy, than find out that they have been cheated on.

At Work: If you're trying to steal staplers and pens from the storage closet, you better hope an ISTJ isn't watching you, because he or she will go straight to HR with details of your villainy. Can you face the disgust in their eyes as they try to process why someone would steal from the company that they themselves love so much? ISTJs aren't perfect by a long shot, but they, at least, aren't thieves and liars.

16. Cares deeply for family and community

Positive: The family-oriented, community-oriented individual is more than just an individual – if they're anything like the ISTJ, then they're practically a one-person movement who values familial ties, loyalty, sticking together through thick and thin and rallying to the aid of others who need it. This is the person who will kick off a fund for a family whose house burned down – by making their own, generous contribution as an example.

Negative: As secure and happy as a family and community can be because of the strength of others who hold it together, it can be a little oppressive at times. A head of household or community pillar can find a little power feeds into an otherwise dormant ego, so that their benevolence starts to become something more like tyranny, disguised as "what's best for this family/community." ISTJs genuinely care, but can be blind to their own short-comings.

In Relationships: It's true that ISTJs value their alone time, but they would never let it threaten the bonds of their family or community. As spouses, INTJs are solely devoted, and as parents, ISTJs want to give their kids every opportunity to succeed, especially if they themselves grew up with little or less.

At Work: ISTJs might be willing to stay late at work, but only if it doesn't coincide with something they promised their kids they'd be present for. Yet because they are such model employees in all other ways – and because they tend to rise among the ranks so that they're in a position where they can delegate the work to others – this shouldn't prove to be much of a problem. In fact, a lot of bosses and coworkers would find it endearing.

17. Providers for themselves and their families

Positive: ISTJs tend to feel blessed that they have the skills and the talent to provide for themselves and their families. It's part duty, of course, especially if they have children, but it is also a real pleasure for them to see their hard work turn into stability and security. More than that, when they see their spouses and children enjoying themselves on a vacation or absolutely thrilled on Christmas morning, it's enough to make this stoic personality type tear up.

Negative: It's a pleasure for ISTJs until it isn't. Hopefully, most of them don't reach the point where the stakes get so high – their families are accustomed to a certain way of life, and anything less would be perceived as the ISTJ's failure – that the stress wears away at them and drains them of their happiness. But it is a distinct possibility, and no one should have to shoulder such all-encompassing responsibility.

In Relationships: The new boyfriend or girlfriend of the ISTJ might suddenly find themselves feeling like a prince or princess, because their mate is a most generous soul to the people they love. What they have to keep in mind, however, as the relationship progresses, is that the ISTJ can't be the only one giving; relationships and marriage are best when both parties are equal.

At Work: There are a lot of reasons why the ISTJ works so hard on the job, but a huge part of it is their sense of duty in providing for the ones they love, while also pleasing themselves by reaching their own personal goals. ISTJs aren't looking for a flashy lifestyle necessarily, but they do tend to end up in well-paying careers where advancement is common.

18. Prepares for the worst

Positive: Do you have that friend who seems to carry everything in her purse? You need a screwdriver, for instance, and voila, she magically produces one from a pocket in her shoulder bag! She could very well be an ISTJ, whose firm sense of practicality enables them to think ahead for any and every mishap, so that they are never caught off guard in a disaster.

Negative: Aside from the comical moment when you have to tell your ISTJ friend that they cannot pack a ratchet in their checked bag in the event of a plane crash near a deserted island (they have seen Castaway, after all), there's the fact that ISTJs can be rather gloom-and-doom about the world. If there's a Debbie Downer in your group, they are probably an ISTJ, a natural pessimist.

In Relationships: In the event of a terrible tragedy, the widow of an ISTJ might discover that her husband took out a secret life insurance policy, so that she and the kids are provided for for the rest of their lives. This is the kind of thoughtful and practical mindset that the ISTJ brings to their relationships.

At Work: The reliable ISTJ is the first person everyone runs to when something goes awry, because without a doubt, they have backed up that file or held onto a seemingly inconsequential document or created the crisis plan. ISTJs are hard workers, but they are also *smart* workers.

19. Comfortable and fun around family and friends

Positive: ISTJs can't be all buttoned-up and fusty 24/7; they're human, and they have to let their hair down once in a while. The people who see this fun-loving side of the ISTJ are usually their closest friends and family, and it's really a huge compliment to anyone who gets to witness the ISTJ in casual clothes, laughing, cracking jokes and having a few beers.

Negative: It's not that the face that ISTJs show to everyone else is nasty or mean in any way – they believe in the Golden Rule, after all – but until someone is accepted into the ISTJ's inner circle, they can expect to be held at a rather chilly arm's length. For people who would rather just be fun and comfortable right off the bat, this type of behavior can be extremely off-putting, and it may even end friendships before they even start.

In Relationships: The mate of the ISTJ sees a side of their partner that no one else does, because on top of their relaxed version of themselves, there is also the romantic. Specific personalities can differ from ISTJ to ISTJ, but their partners and families can expect silliness, warm humor and maybe even a surprise or two at holidays or birthdays (well-planned out for weeks in advance, of course).

At Work: If ISTJs work in an environment where they are putting their heads together with others or bouncing ideas off one another between bouts of independent work, then there is a good chance that they will let their guard down a bit on the job. It will likely be a long process, but if they stay at one place for long enough, their more open side should come out.

20. Believes in the letter of the law and tradition

Positive: Most of us can walk in a park without fear of getting kidnapped or attacked because people like the ISTJs uphold the law on both a micro and macro level. Their belief and their faith in the justice of the law and the strengths of tradition protect families, create close-knit communities and ensure that bad people are punished accordingly.

Negative: Sometimes the laws are broken. Sometimes, tradition is outdated. But ISTJs aren't often going to see that – in fact, they might not want to see it that way, because they like the old ways. Change is scary, but ISTJs in particular are not very adaptable, so this is a personality type that can end up on the wrong side of history.

In Relationships: Ever met the kid of a cop? They're usually the most rambunctious trouble-makers. The reason is usually because people who believe deeply in the sanctity of law and tradition tend to be hyper-vigilant about it at home, and their kids feel suffocated. Yet the lessons about wrong and right usually do stick, so that when children mature, they blossom into good adults.

At Work: Expect the ISTJ to be morally outraged when a group of coworkers makes a habit of sneaking back into the office 10 minutes late after lunch. Sure, it's just 10 minutes, but the ISTJ was back on the job at the appropriate time – so why can't everyone else? They might seem like stick-in-the-muds, but businesses need structure to stay afloat.

21. Has difficulty telling people no and ends up overwhelmed

Positive: It should come as no surprise if ISTJs like to stay busy and generally take a great deal of pleasure in saying "yes" and putting their skills to work for others. As thinkers and judgers, ISTJs are methodical and organized, born to manage and leave things better than they found them. They don't mind a full plate, because helping others helps make the community stronger.

Negative: Their dutiful personality does mean that the ISTJ can be confronted by someone who needs something and, standing there face-to-face with a person who has come for help, they simply cannot say "no," despite knowing that there is so much for them to do already. This almost certainly leads the "me-time"-craving ISTJ utterly defeated and overwhelmed at some point.

In Relationships: ISTJs are incredibly devoted to their families, but it is possible for them to neglect those they love while they are off in the service of others. This can be as major as a tour of duty overseas or as minor as helping to build a parade float for the local VFW. The families of ISTJs will understand for the most part, but this personality type must be careful to give them due attention.

At Work: Because the ISTJ knows that a company is only as strong as its weakest link, if a coworker comes to them for help or the boss throws an extra project their way, the ISTJ just can't turn it away. For them, it is their responsibility and their duty as a good employee to build up the company to be the very best it can be, because the ISTJ is inextricably linked to it.

22. Supports the conventional

Positive: The conventional is good, because it's reliable, predictable and comforting, and the ISTJ takes to traditional conventions like a fish to water. A conventional way of life might not be for everyone, but those around the ISTJ know that this individual embodies all of the good that comes with it, as they strive to improve their world and their environment by being a decent person.

Negative: Conventions exist because the same act or belief has been repeated over and over again, but the times are a-changing, and if the ISTJ can't change with them – at least the littlest bit – they risk being viewed as a bigot or something equally unsavory. Progress should not be the ISTJ's enemy – they should be able to appreciate the logical reasoning that including more people is better.

In Relationships: Of all the personality types, ISTJs are most likely to conform to traditional gender norms when it comes to their relationships. This means that ISTJ men believe that they should work outside of the home and provide for the family, while the women view their place as the hearth and home. There is absolutely nothing wrong with this, and many ISTJs are perfectly happy and healthy in these roles.

At Work: Perhaps ISTJs will support a change of paint color in the break room, but for the most part, they want their work environment to stay the way it is. This can cause some friction with younger or more liberal members of the staff, but it does tend to make ISTJs popular with their bosses.

23. Prefers to work by themselves

Positive: If there is one thing to be said for ISTJs, it's that they know who they are. Some people spend decades trying to figure out their true preferences, but not the ISTJs. And these personality types recognize that because of their introverted aspects, they are most productive and efficient when they work on their projects as singles, not as part of a team. When they are given the freedom to work things out for themselves, the job will get done right and fast.

Negative: Some situations in life absolutely require you to be able to work with other people as part of a team, and trying to get out of it can make ISTJs look like antisocial jerks. To clarify, they certainly are not, but when only one person is protesting and pouting and making a bit of a scene, that guy or gal looks immature.

In Relationships: If you ask your ISTJ spouse to build a bookshelf for you, back off. In fact, you might want to leave the house entirely and go find something else to do until they finish, because if you so much as peek in without an invitation, your ISTJ partner will shoo you right out lest you try to lend a hand (a.k.a. "mangle their progress").

At Work: The ISTJ preference for working as a lone wolf is evident in the types of careers that they pursue. Even if they are part of a larger office, you can bet they only took the job if it was a relatively isolated position with not a lot of team projects. Plus, ISTJs make good managers, so as they move up the ranks, they are given more independence.

24. Not adventurous

Positive: People die occasionally because of sky-diving accidents. They contract deadly diseases while roaming foreign countries. They drown while on ambitious and ill-advised boating voyages. ISTJs weigh their options and prefer to avoid the possibility of a painful and slow death by sticking to the places they know and not going traipsing off on some wild adventure.

Negative: A life lived without taking risks can be a very dull life, indeed. No one has actually done a study or anything, but it is possible that when ISTJs are on their deathbed, and they're thinking about what they would have done differently, it's possible that they wish they had taken more chances and seen the wider world and all that it has to offer.

In Relationships: Free spirits seeking a partner in crime had better look elsewhere, because the ISTJ isn't interested in picking up at a moment's notice and heading for the hills (or beach or jungle or wherever). However, that doesn't mean ISTJs aren't interested in travel at all – they would just prefer the trip be planned out well in advance with no surprises.

At Work: ISTJs are exactly the types of people who do their best work at a desk or in an office. Other personalities need to be out in the thick of things, among people and chasing down a story or a lead, but ISTJs would prefer if the most adventurous thing that happens during their work day is that they have a hamburger instead of a salad during the lunch hour.

25. Prefers personal responsibility

Positive: Without a doubt, ISTJs will own to their actions. If they are the cause of a problem or issue, ISTJs won't try to point fingers or reassign the blame – that is not only cowardly in their eyes, but completely lacking in integrity. They bow their heads and acknowledge their role in the mishap so that no one else takes the fall for them.

Negative: Unfortunately, ISTJs rather naively expect everyone else to do the same, but of course, the world is populated with people who would rather watch others burn than themselves go down in flames. ISTJs can find themselves reeling in horror as someone else throws them under the bus, but sadly, they are the ones who are out of touch with human nature.

In Relationships: ISTJs in relationships will absolutely own to their faults, as long as their partner is prepared to do the same. If, however, they find that their mate is prone to deflecting and pointing the blame elsewhere, it simply won't work out. This is another reason ISTJs do well when they team up – their values are just so strong and such an integral part of their lives.

At Work: If the ISTJ somehow got stuck doing a group project at work, and someone didn't pull their weight, it will eat away at this personality type for days, possibly weeks. This is part of the reason it's so important that ISTJs be able to work on their own. However, even if employees do work independently, someone else's blunder could mess everything up and ISTJs expect that person to own it.

26. More comfortable in positions of authority

Positive: A lot of people don't like telling others what to do, but the ISTJ knows that his or her ideas are as logical and well-reasoned as ideas can get, so they are confident when placed at the head of a group (it sure beats being told what to do by others, as far as they're concerned).

Negative: If the ISTJ is simply another underling in a group, even if it's just a team baking effort, they can get pretty resentful when someone else tries to boss them around – because, after all, they have Grandma's award-winning brownie recipe *right here*. ISTJs make it known through surly demeanor when they are not happy at being directed by people they perceive as less qualified.

In Relationships: Male and female ISTJs can be total know-it-alls, but the men in particular tend to establish themselves as the "heads of household," the major bread-winners and the ones with the final say in most decisions. And they seek women who prefer this arrangement as well.

At Work: ISTJs make wonderful managers and leaders, as long as their underlings don't mind being given directions just once, without much elaboration. ISTJs are no-nonsense, and their practical, pragmatic personalities allow them to operate in the work environment with a calm, composed confidence that practically begs for a position of authority.

27. Knowledgeable about the truth, a good source for facts.

Positive: If your local bar has a trivia night, grab your closest ISTJ friend and bring them in, because they will help your team dominate. ISTJs are naturally information sponges – they're not just sitting around staring at the ceiling during their alone time, they usually prefer to read – and it makes them very intelligent on a number of topics.

Negative: As mentioned, ISTJs can be know-it-alls, and they will defend their belief that they are right even if it means devolving into a shouting match with Grandma. Luckily, we live in a world where most matters of trivia can be solved by checking the Internet, but if no one has their phone on them, ISTJs can make matters quite tense.

In Relationships: ISTJs value tradition, but they also place a high premium on intelligence and a broad education. This means they themselves come to a relationship with knowledge and skills, and they are well-matched with people who have their own complementary set of knowledge/skills. Together, the ISTJ and his/her partner can be a formidable team of truth.

At Work: ISTJs are probably the people who can be used to settle disputes or answer a quick question in a jiffy – they just have that special talent for remembering a lot of information, even the stuff that doesn't seem too important. Their coworkers and their bosses know that this is a mind to be reckoned with – and picked, now and then.

28. Enjoys analysis

Positive: ISTJs don't just analyze for the sake of analysis – they'd like to see the world become a better place ("better" usually means more in-tune with their value system, but the sentiment is well-meant). So they take their extraordinary gifts for seeing beyond what's on the surface and figure out how to make improvements.

Negative: People sometimes just tell it like it is. Situations are exactly what they appear to be. An analysis is usually necessary and can normally find room for improvement, but not always. And if the ISTJ is spending time trying to think it through – without even realizing it – then that is time wasted on something that is obvious and opaque.

In Relationships: Analysis isn't a chore for the ISTJ – they rather like it, and relationships are some of the most fun situations out there to think about. Male or female, the ISTJ has to be careful not to go too far down the rabbit hole in a "What did that sentence mean?" kind of way; they should instead just learn to ask their partner to clarify.

At Work: The ISTJ enjoyment of analysis has a big impact on the kinds of jobs that they pursue. You won't find an ISTJ making a living with a paintbrush – but you will find them analyzing IT systems to make them more secure for companies who have sensitive customer information.

29. Not naturally in tune with emotions

Positive: Emotions can take fraught situations to a whole other level of chaotic, but the ISTJ keeps their feelings on lockdown. Not only that, a lot of people feed off of the emotions of others, so in a situation where there is anger, both parties sense each other's fury and the ire grows. The ISTJ effectively prohibits this phenomenon by not giving out or sensing emotions.

Negative: There are plenty of times when being in-tune with emotion will lead to a more satisfying experience for all, such as helping impoverished people at a shelter. It could be that ISTJs volunteer to work in a soup kitchen because it's their civic duty, not because they feel empathy for others.

In Relationships: It is very difficult for ISTJs who find themselves paired with feeling types, and there is enough disconnect that it might not end up working out. Thinking types either need excessive patient feeling counterparts or they should just stick with people whose personalities are more aligned with theirs.

At Work: ISTJ's lack of emotional response on the job can keep stressful situations from escalating, but at the same time, this personality type is more prone to say a sharp, critical word to someone and never realize that they did anything wrong – unless someone else tells them or they find their coworker crying in a supply closet.

30. Strives for perfection

Positive: Part of the thinking and judging aspects involves a strong streak of perfectionism, which the ISTJ most certainly has. It's not always personal gratification for them (it's certainly not the need for attention), but rather the sense that it's their duty as citizens. And many of us do benefit from their attention to detail, whether we realize it or not.

Negative: Perfectionism is a double-edged sword, because in some cases, zero error is simply not possible, and the ISTJ can drive him/herself crazy trying to attain it. And when they can't, they beat themselves up over it, needlessly.

In Relationships: Not everyone's idea of perfection in a relationship matches the ISTJ's, but these personality types have earnest aspiration on their side. They genuinely want to be the best partners and parents that they can be, and they will do it the only way they know how – through discipline, patience and persistence.

At Work: ISTJs probably get on their coworker's nerves without realizing it, because the work they do is just so high-quality. In a lot of instances it is effortless, but that big, stressful project that's on such a tight deadline can have them quaking in their boots come turn-in day.

31. Does not freely give compliments

Positive: We live in a world where people get congratulated just for showing up. Well the ISTJs, much like your war veteran grandpa, just don't believe in putting on the kid gloves. A lot of people today could use a big dose of the truth, no matter how hard, and the ISTJ is at the fore of this movement, withholding their compliments until someone has really earned it.

Negative: ISTJs have a reputation for being overly critical, and while it is true that people need to learn how to earn their accolades, the ISTJ needs to find the right balance between doling out tough love and being downright stingy. They'll get more done if there are more people on their side.

In Relationships: Partners and children of ISTJs know that when their mate or parent gives out a compliment they have done one outstanding job. While it may be felt that the ISTJ is hyper-critical even among the people they love (and who love them), there is nothing like that feeling when they say, "Wow, nice job."

At Work: The ISTJ in a position of authority is a tough cookie, an unsentimental boss who expects perfection as if by rote. But like with family members and friends, the compliments that come from them mean more than a million bucks.

32. Uncomfortable expressing emotions around strangers or acquaintances

Positive: There are really a lot of benefits to keeping one's own council and not revealing the emotion behind one's eyes, and the ISTJ appreciates them all. Why muddy matters with an overly maudlin cry or a flash of temper? These displays are uncomfortable for the ISTJ, and they can be uncomfortable for the strangers, too.

Negative: Someone the ISTJ met at a social function might walk away from the encounter completely oblivious of the fact that the stolid person with whom they were chatting was actually incredibly excited to meet and cannot wait to see them again. These are the pitfalls of a perpetual poker-face.

In Relationships: Thankfully, most ISTJ partners and families don't see that more closed-off person – they get the very best of the ISTJ, with all the humor and playfulness and humor. It serves to remind them of how lucky they are to have someone so committed to providing.

At Work: If their coworkers are close enough, ISTJs will come out of their shell a bit – they may even come out a lot and really show their workplace who they are. One hopes for this more open persona, because there is no harm in being friendly and fun while getting things done.

33. Expresses themselves through actions over words

Positive: Actions speak louder than words for the ISTJ, who is demonstrative and thoughtful. Their sensing aspect gives a grounded practicality to what they do for others, and one cannot help but be touched when the ISTJ gets up half an hour early to shovel the elderly neighbor's driveway and then runs away before he can be thanked.

Negative: Men are notorious for "missing signals," but people of both genders can find themselves scratching their head when the ISTJ's actions – which they themselves believed to be sending an obvious message – go unnoticed. ISTJs have to learn when it's necessary to speak up because some people only respond to a forceful word.

In Relationships: The ISTJ partner says "I love you" sparingly, but their obvious devotion is shown in the way they buy their mate a pair of expensive windshield wipers or in the foot rubs in front of the fireplace. They pay attention and they deliver in few words and much action.

At Work: Expect not to hear a peep out of a disgruntled ISTJ coworkers, but they are not above some passive-aggressive door slamming. Further, you will know when your ISTJ boss is impressed with your work, not because you got a nice announcement to the office – but because you got a big promotion.